DOODLE DO!

This edition published in 2010 by Arcturus Publishing Limited
26/27 Bickels Yard, 151–153 Bermondsey Street,
London SE1 3HA

Copyright © 2010 Arcturus Publishing Limited

All rights reserved. No part of this publication may be reproduced, stored in a retrieval system, or transmitted, in any form or by any means, electronic, mechanical, photocopying, recording or otherwise, without written permission in accordance with the provisions of the Copyright Act 1956 (as amended). Any person or persons who do any unauthorised act in relation to this publication may be liable to criminal prosecution and civil claims for damages.

ISBN: 978-1-84837-510-9
CH001418EN

Created by Small World Design
Additional design by Omnipress

Printed in India

What else is he juggling with?

What is lurking in Nessie's lair?

Mark on the island's other deadly dangers.

Give them really wild hairstyles.

Mmm... it's your favourite cake!

Finish the time machine.

Who is hiding in the dark, spooky wood?

What are they building?

Draw the other members of the alien's family.

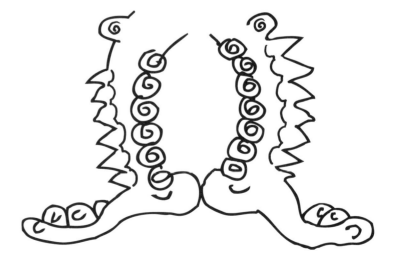

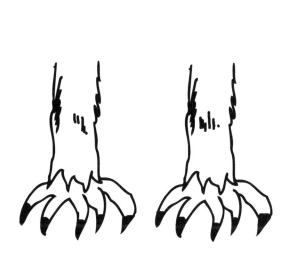
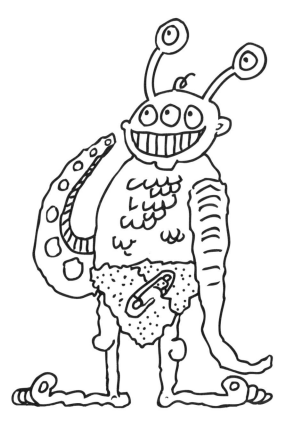

Who won the monster beauty contest?

Draw the goldfish you won at the fair.

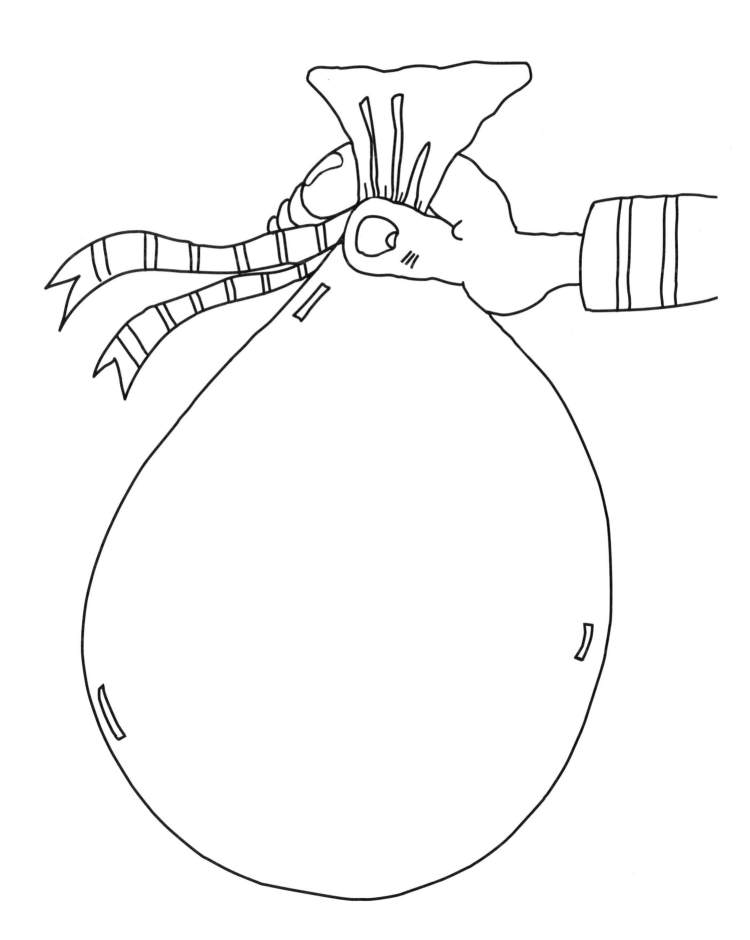

Draw the surfers catching the big wave.

What's the fireman rescuing?

It's the ice cream of your dreams!

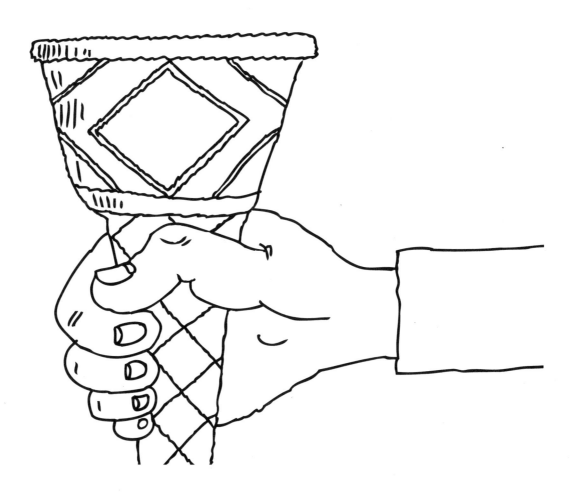

What has the magician pulled out of his hat?

The ghost detector doesn't lie... but where's the ghost?

Draw what the magpie has in her nest.

It's the portrait of Dracula's grandfather!

Looks like he's in for a bumpy landing!

What team does he support?

Draw the man in the moon.

At last! The knights have reached the castle!

Complete the clown.

Give these ducks some woolly jumpers!

Finish the mole's house.

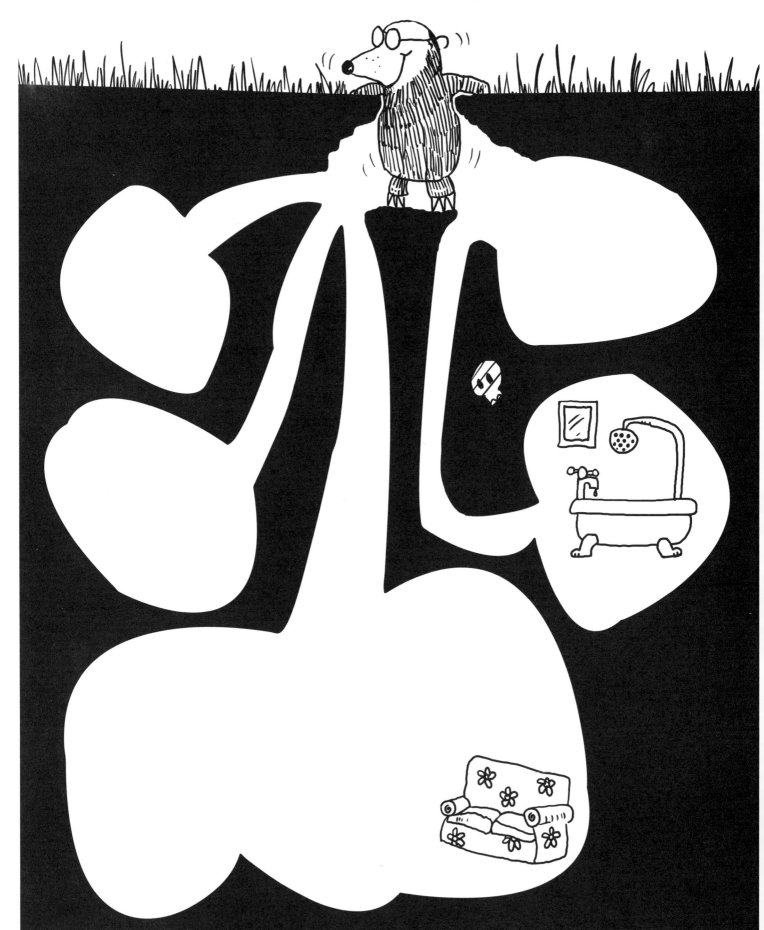

What has interrupted her beauty sleep?

Who else is balancing on the tightrope?

Yikes! It's a giant spider!

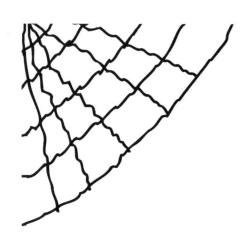

What sort of baby is the stork delivering?

Draw the animals they've spotted on safari.

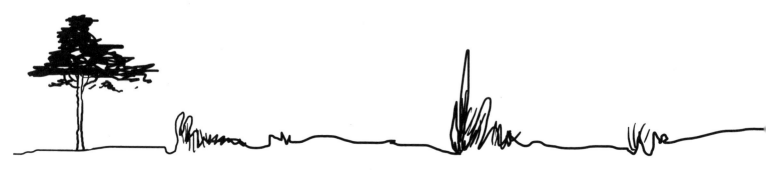

It's a house made of sweets! Add as many as you can.

Why has this camel got the hump?

Finish the caveman's family.

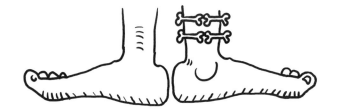

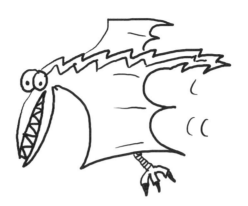

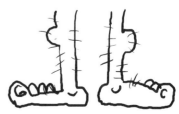

The explorer has discovered a new land.

What did the young witch turn her teacher into?

Give the superhero a super suit!